FLOWER ORIGAMI

By Joost Langeveld

THUNDER BAY
P·R·E·S·S

Thunder Bay Press
An imprint of the Baker & Taylor Publishing Group
10350 Barnes Canyon Road, San Diego, CA 92121
www.thunderbaybooks.com

To see more origami designs by Joost Langeveld and to view educational videos, visit his web site: www.joostlangeveldorigami.nl.

ISBN-13: 978-1-60710-280-9
ISBN-10: 1-60710-280-3

Printed in China.
1 2 3 4 5 15 14 13 12 11

Table Of Contents

Origami Terms

Valley fold

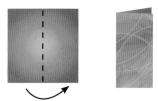

Mountain fold

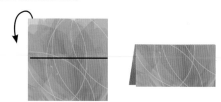

Fold in direction
of arrow

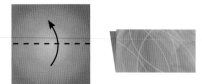

Turn model over

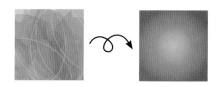

Fold and unfold

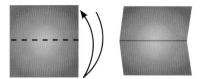

Rotate model

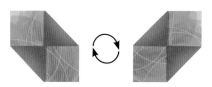

Push/apply pressure

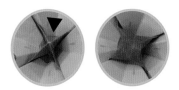

Inside reverse fold

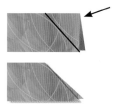

Next stage   ⟶

Stem

1 Cut long strips 1 inch wide from green origami paper. Glue two strips together at one edge to make a strip long enough for a stem. Allow to dry.

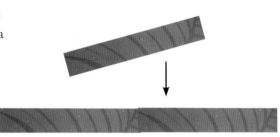

2 Fold one edge in partway, then fold the opposite edge in, overlapping the first.

3 Unfold. Insert a piece of floral stem wire, folded down to fit, between the layers. Glue the stem shut. Allow to dry.

Preliminary Base

1. Position the paper so that the patterned side is face up. Mountain fold the paper in half horizontally and vertically. Unfold after each fold.

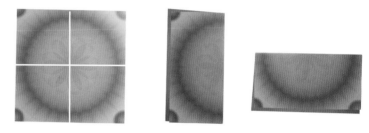

2. Valley fold the paper in half along both diagonals, unfolding after each fold.

3. Then push two opposite sides together and flatten the model. This is the completed preliminary base.

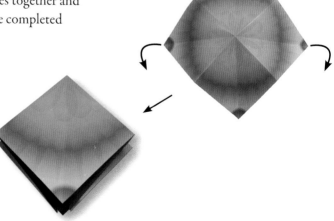

Blintz Base

1 With the patterned side face up, valley fold along
the diagonals. Unfold after each fold. Then,
mountain fold as shown. Turn the model over.

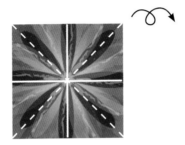

2 Valley fold each corner to the center.

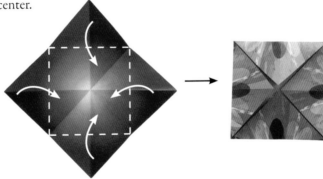

3 Fold corners back out partway as shown.

Pansy

1   Valley fold horizontally and vertically. Mountain fold along the diagonals. Unfold after each fold.

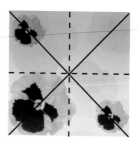

2   Align the edge of a mountain crease with an existing valley fold. Repeat on the opposite side.

3   Pleat the bottom of the flower: push edges A and B under the paper, mountain folding as shown.

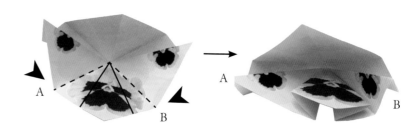

4 Hold the flower in a cone shape and turn it over.
Squeeze the tip together to narrow it.

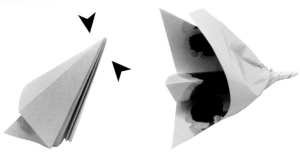

5 Spread the petals out a bit.

6 Mountain fold the tip of the top petal.

7 Fold back the points of the side petals.

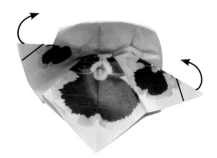

8 Fold the bottom tip under.

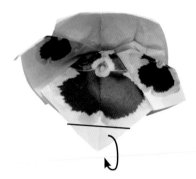

9 Press point C—the center of the bottom edge—down in an inside reverse fold.

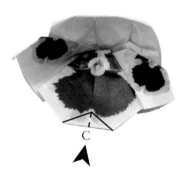

C

10 Mountain fold the corners shown to round the petals and separate them.

Tulip

1 Start with a blintz base (see page 7) and valley fold along dashed lines shown. Turn the model over.

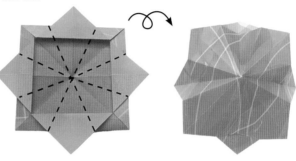

2 Mountain fold edges A and B to the center crease.

3 Repeat step 2 on the other three sides of the model.

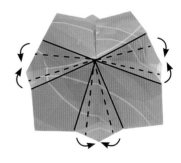

4 Turn the model over.

5 Holding the model lightly from the bottom, start to collapse it into a cone.

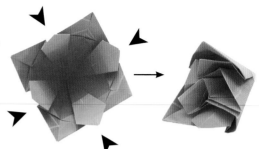

6 Turn the model over to work on the tip. Valley fold along the dashed line shown.

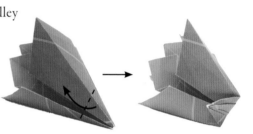

7 Holding the tip down with your thumb, valley fold along the dashed line shown.

8 Press the model out a little at the bottom from the inside.

Large Spiky Leaf

1. Valley fold along the diagonal. Unfold.

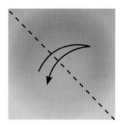

2. Narrow the model into a long, spiky leaf by folding the edges to the center crease in a series of valley folds.

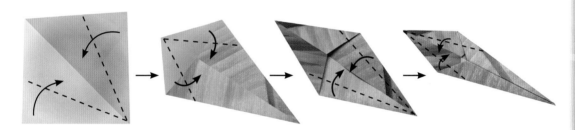

3. Turn the model over, then curl a little for the finished leaf.

Use this leaf with other flowers: narcissus, daffodil, iris.

Anthurium

1. Mountain fold along the diagonal and unfold. Turn the paper over.

2. Valley fold the edges to the center crease.

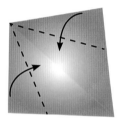

3. Mountain fold the tip to the back of the model, then turn the model over.

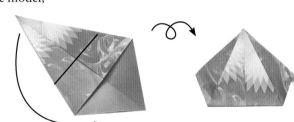

4. Valley fold along the dashed line and unfold.

5 Inside reverse fold the sides, folding the top part from edges to the center crease and pivoting at the crease made in step 4, so that the part stands up.

6 Valley fold the tip.

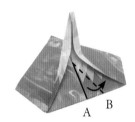

7 Pull point A past point B, mountain and valley folding as indicated.

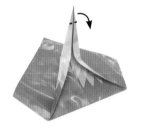

8 Mountain fold the lower edges. Mountain fold the upper edges to round out the flower.

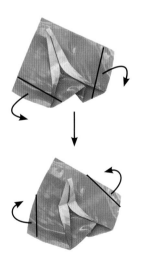

Bluebell

1 Start with a preliminary base (see page 6). Valley fold the edges to the center crease and unfold.

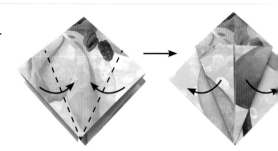

2 Pull point A out and up, creasing along dashed line shown.

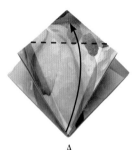

A

3 Using existing creases, press the model flat.

4 Turn the model over and repeat steps 1 to 3 on the other side.

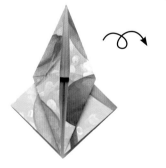

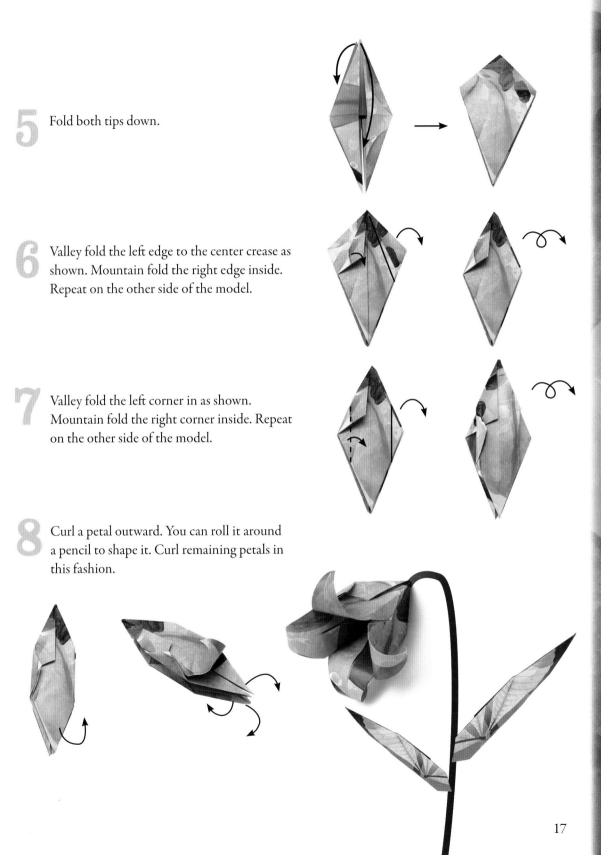

5 Fold both tips down.

6 Valley fold the left edge to the center crease as shown. Mountain fold the right edge inside. Repeat on the other side of the model.

7 Valley fold the left corner in as shown. Mountain fold the right corner inside. Repeat on the other side of the model.

8 Curl a petal outward. You can roll it around a pencil to shape it. Curl remaining petals in this fashion.

17

Small Spiky Leaf

1. Turn the paper face down.

2. Valley fold along the dashed lines. The tips can overlap a little.

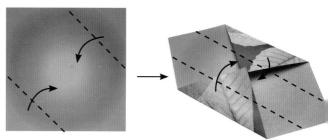

3. Valley fold along the dashed lines again, creating a pointed tip. Turn the model over.

Try this leaf with other flowers: carnation, lily.

Carnation

1. Start with a blintz base folded through to step 2.
Valley fold the corners out ⅓ of the way.

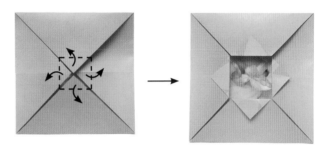

2. Valley fold the inner edges to the outer edges.

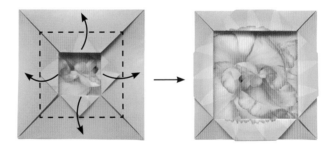

3. Mountain fold the corners along the folded edges.

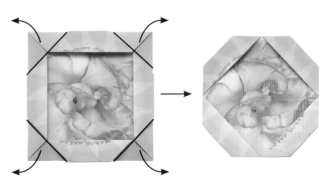

4　Keeping this side up, crumple the model in your hand, the unfold it back to the view in step 3.

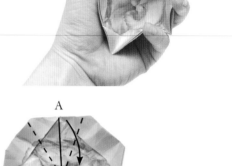

5　Make valley folds as shown. Mountain fold vertically. Pull points A and B past each other in the center to form a cone.

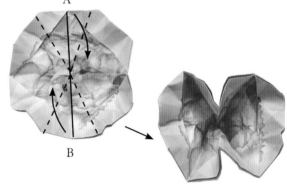

6　Hold the cone from the sides as shown. Turn the model to work on the bottom.

7　Squeeze the bottom to narrow and give the tip a good twist.

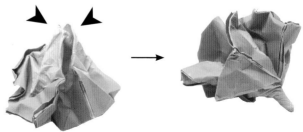

8 Turn the flower back to work on the top. Separate the layers to give the flower a rufflly effect.

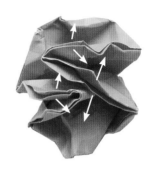

9 Mountain or valley fold some of the edges. This will help it keep its ruffly shape.

10 Adjust the outer layers as desired.

Rose

1 Start with a preliminary base (see page 6).

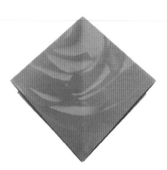

2 Valley fold the edges to the center crease and unfold.

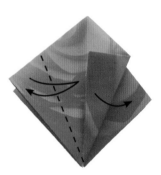

3 Pull point A out and up, valley folding along the dashed line.

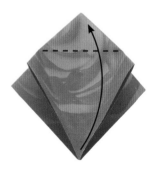

4 Using existing creases, flatten the sides as shown.

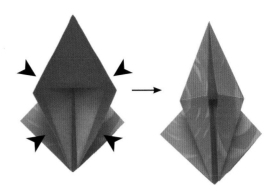

5 Repeat steps 2 to 4 on the backside of the model.

6 Fold the flaps down.

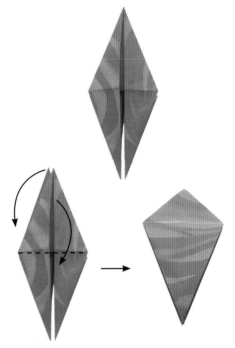

7 Fold the top flap like an accordion: make a series of valley folds as shown, then mountain fold the tip.

8 Repeat step 7 on the other three flaps.

9 Working inside the model, inside reverse-fold the corner indicated by pushing the corner to the inside of the layers. Repeat with the other corners.

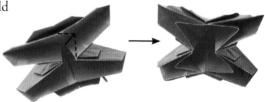

10 Mountain fold the side edges and tuck them out of sight. Make the same folds on the other side of the model.

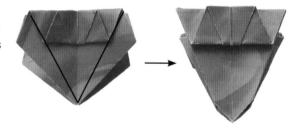

11 Holding the model in your hand, squeeze from all sides to open up the inner folds. Press the large corner shown into the inside reverse fold.

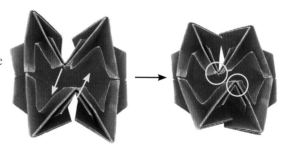

12 Repeat on the other side.

13 Squeeze the tip of the flower flat from all sides. Then give it a good twist.

Spade-Shaped Leaf

1 Turn the paper so it is face down.

2 Valley fold along the diagonal. Unfold.

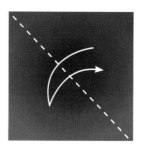

3 Valley fold along the dashed lines shown.

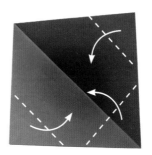

4 Narrow the tip by valley folding along the dashed lines shown.

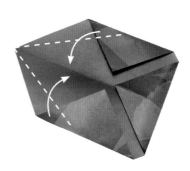

5 Inside reverse fold the base of the leaf (pull point A up).

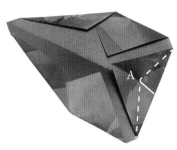

6 Turn the model over.

7 Pinch the tip between two fingers. Crumple the leaf a bit with your hands.

Water Lily

1 Start with a blintz base (see page 7) folded through step 2. Valley fold the corners to the center.

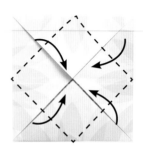

2 Valley fold the new corners to the center.

3 Valley fold the new corners to the center one more time.

4 Pull out the four top petals so they stand up.

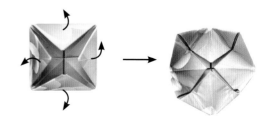

5 Pull up a corner from the layer beneath.

6 Repeat with the remaining corners.

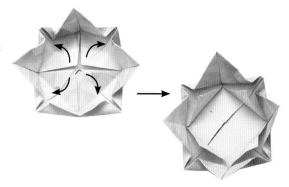

7 Pull up the corners from the next layer down and press them against the standing petals.

8 Curl up the corner tips of the final layer.

Azalea

1 Start with a blintz base (see page 7). Valley fold along the dashed lines shown.

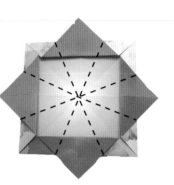

2 Fold three corners to the inside as indicated. Turn the model over.

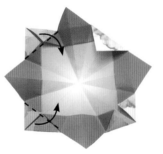

3 Pull point B to the left past point A, using existing creases.

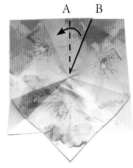

4 Repeat with points C and D, E and F, using existing creases.

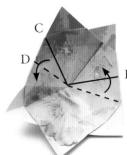

5 Make mountain and valley folds as indicated. Pull point G to the right, just past point H. Repeat on the opposite side with points I and J.

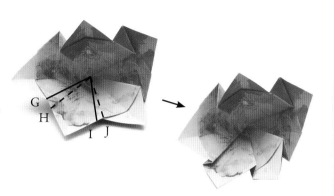

6 Holding the model upside-down, pinch the bottom into a point. Turn the model over.

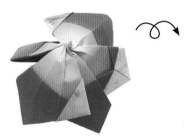

7 Pinch the tip of a petal between two fingers into a point as shown. Repeat with remaining petals.

Sunflower

1 Start with a blintz base (see page 7). Turn the model over. Valley fold along dashed lines shown.

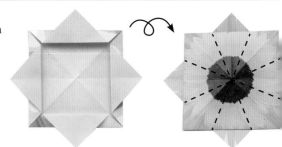

2 Fold points A and B to C using existing creases. Continue alternating valley and mountain folds to collapse the model into a diamond shape and flatten.

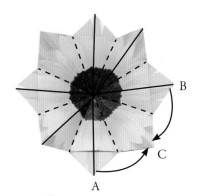

3 Valley fold along the dashed line, then reverse the crease to a mountain fold. This makes a guide for later. Unfold the model to the same view as seen in step 2. Turn the model over.

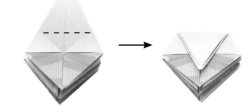

4 Mountain fold along existing creases made in step 3, then press the center of the model down.

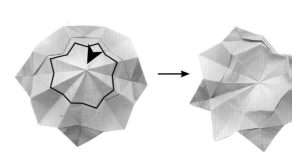

5 Press inward between the points while sharpening the mountain creases.

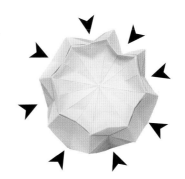

6 Turn the model over.

7 Separate the petals with pleats: mountain fold as shown, then bring the folded edge past the existing valley fold. Repeat with the remaining petals.

8 Fold a petal out as shown. Repeat with remaining petals.

Violet

1 Start with a blintz base (see page 7). Then turn the paper over.

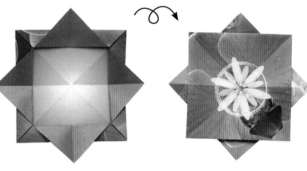

2 Valley fold as indicated along the dashed lines.

3 Fold points A and B to C, using existing creases. Continue alternating valley and mountain folds to collapse the model into a diamond shape and flatten.

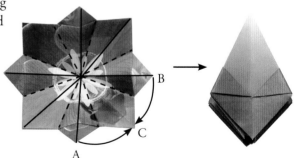

4 Make a valley fold over the dashed line and unfold. Mountain fold over the same line, then unfold the model entirely. The side with the yellow center is face down.

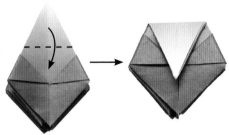

5 Mountain fold along the solid lines, using existing creases to guide you. Then sink the center of the model.

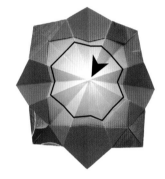

6 Press the model inward at all points indicated so the model will collapse and flatten. See the photo in step 7 for proper view.

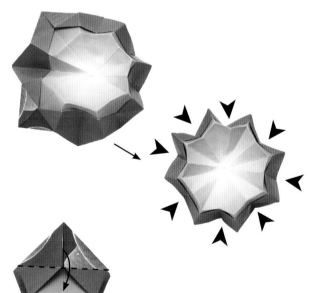

7 Fold the point down as shown.

8 Make an inside reverse fold as shown through the top layers by pulling the center point (D) down. This is done to hide an extra petal.

9 Repeat steps 7 and 8 to hide two more extra petals.

10 Pull point E to the left and crease to make a wide, flat petal. Now fold the petal back so it is perpendicular to the center.

11 Repeat with remaining points to make four more flat, wide petals. Press the center of the flower a little to flatten.

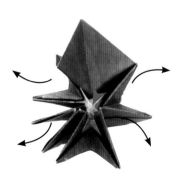

12 Mountain fold the tip of each petal.

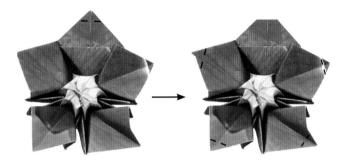

Primrose

1 Start with a blintz base (see page 7).
   Turn the model over.

2 Valley fold along the dashed lines
   and unfold.

3 Collapse the model: start by pulling
   points A and B to point C. Then continue
   alternating mountain and valley folds
   along existing creases so the model folds
   up into a diamond shape and flatten.

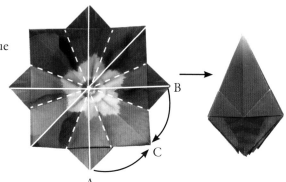

4 Valley fold the tip to the raw edge. Then reverse the fold to sharpen the creases.

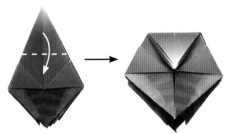

5 Unfold the model to the same view as step 3. Turn the model over.

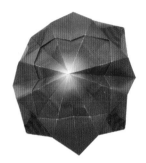

6 Mountain fold along existing creases, then push the center in to sink it.

7 Sharpen the mountain creases and press inward between the points as shown. Then turn the model over.

8 Pleat the petals to separate them: mountain crease as shown, pulling the mountain fold past the valley fold. Repeat with remaining petals.

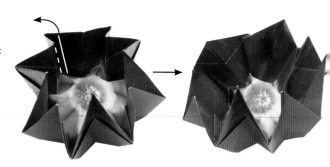

9 Press on a petal to fold it out. Repeat with remaining petals.

10 Fold a petal tip back as shown. Repeat with remaining petals.

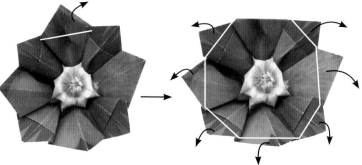

11 Press the edge of a petal down at point D to make an inside reverse fold.

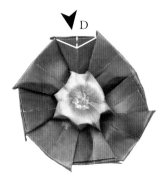

12   Repeat with remaining petals.

13   Press the outer rim of petals away from the flower center.

Dahlia

1 Start with a blintz base (see page 7). Valley fold along the dashed lines shown.

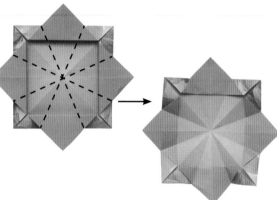

2 Start to collapse the model: fold points A and B to point C, alternating mountain and valley folds. Continue in this fashion until the model is flat.

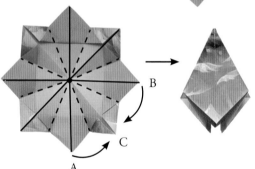

3 Valley fold along dashed lines and unfold.

4 Unfold the model and flatten.

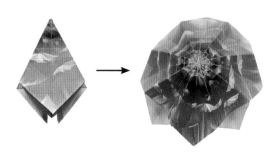

5 Pressing the center down, mountain fold along the outermost ring of creases made in step 3.

6 Valley fold along the next ring of creases, pushing the center up.

7 Mountain fold the third ring of creases, pushing the center down.

8 Valley fold the innermost ring of creases while pushing the center up.

9   Sharpen the folded edges, then turn the
    model on its side to work on the petals.

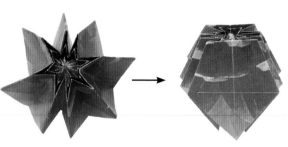

10 Fold the petal up in an inside reverse fold.

11 Fold the same petal back down in an inside
    reverse fold close to the previous one.

12 Make a final inside reverse fold close to the
    previous ones to push the petal tip back up.

13 Repeat steps 10 to 12 on the remaining petals.

14 View from above.

15 Make shallow inside reverse folds along the outer ring of edges.

16 Repeat step 15 on the inner ring of edges.

Lotus

1   Start with a blintz base (see page 7) folded through step 2. Turn the model over.

2   Fold the square into a preliminary base (see page 6). The cut edges should be visible on the outer flaps.

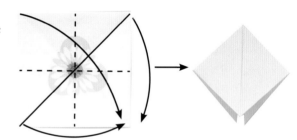

3   Book fold the right flap so it stands up. Press the corner down and squash it flat.

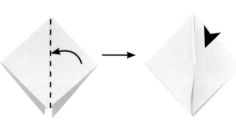

4   Valley fold the edges to the center and unfold.

5 Pull the point A out and up, then flatten along existing creases. Fold the small triangular piece down.

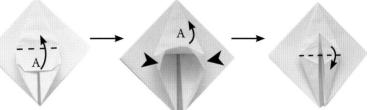

6 Repeat steps 3 to 5 on the other three flaps. Rotate the model 180°.

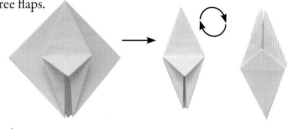

7 Pull the two petals apart, then tuck the triangular piece to the inside. Flatten along existing creases.

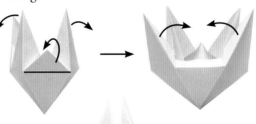

8 Repeat step 7 with the remaining sides.

9 This model requires extra petals. Make the first: valley fold along the dashed line. Then pull the outer layer out and invert, flattening along existing creases.

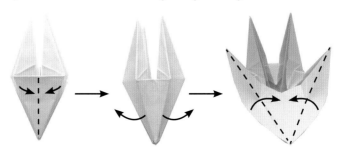

47

10 Fold the extra petal up as shown. Repeat step 9 on the other sides of the model to make a total of four extra petals.

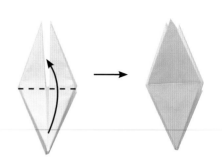

11 Valley fold the tip along the dashed line. Now sharpen the crease by reversing it to a mountain fold. Unfold and turn the model upside down.

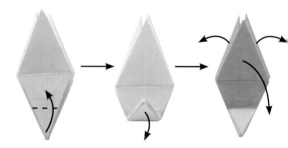

12 Mountain fold along the existing creases.

13 Sink the center point, then start to collapse the model (but not all the way), pressing in along the edges.

14 Crease the edges well and turn the model over.

15 Four of the petals are made from fewer layers; these will be on the inside of the flower. Locate a thinner petal and make valley folds shown.

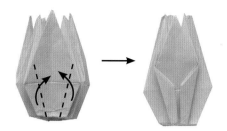

16 Repeat with the other three thin petals.

17 Curl the four thicker petals outward by rolling them around a pencil. Curl the thinner petals inward at the tips.

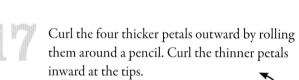

Cherry Blossom

1 Start with a blintz base (see page 7), folded through step 2. Turn the model over.

2 Fold the square into a preliminary base (see page 6). The raw edges should be visible on the outer flaps.

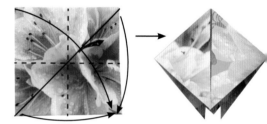

3 Book fold the right flap so it stands up. Press the corner down and squash it flat.

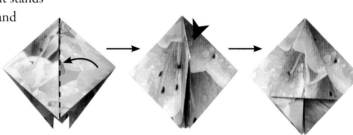

4 Valley fold the edges to the center and unfold.

5 Pull point A out and up, then flatten along existing creases.

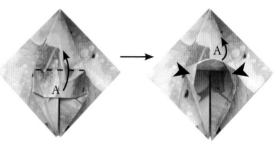

6 Fold the small triangular piece down.

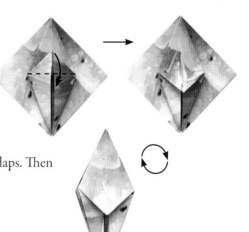

7 Repeat steps 3 to 6 on the other three flaps. Then rotate the model 180°.

8 Pull the two petals outward, then tuck the triangular piece to the inside. Flatten along existing creases. Repeat with remaining petals.

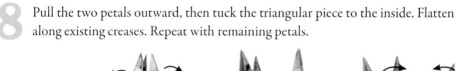

9 To make a fifth petal, valley fold along the dashed line. Then pull the outer layer out and invert, flattening along existing creases.

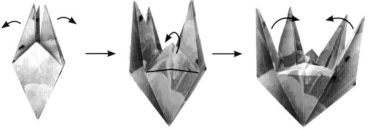

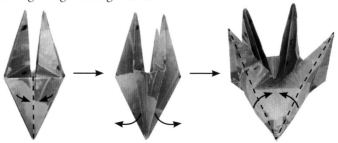

51

10 Fold the extra petal up as shown.

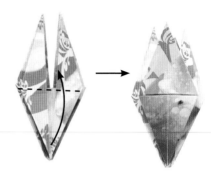

11 Book fold the flaps twice.

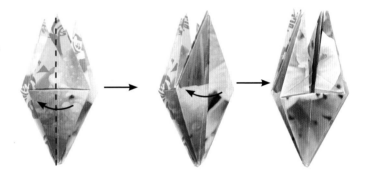

12 Pull point B down to make an inside reverse fold between the petals. Repeat on the same points between the other petals.

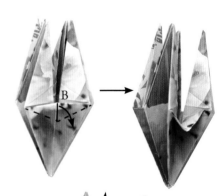

13 Press a petal down, mountain folding as indicated to make corners between petals.

14 Continue pressing petals down and making corners between them until all are pressed out.

15 Fold back each petal tip, then curl each petal back around a pencil.

Hyacinth

1. Start with a blintz base folded through step 2 (see page 7). Turn the model over.

2. Fold the square into a preliminary base. The cut edges should be visible on the outer flaps.

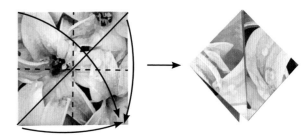

3. Book fold the right flap so it stands up. Press the corner down and squash it flat.

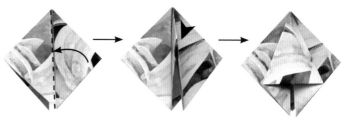

4. Valley fold the edges to the center and unfold.

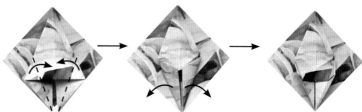

5 Pull point A out and up, then flatten along existing creases.

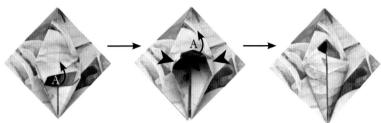

6 Fold the small triangular piece down. Repeat steps 3 to 6 on the other three flaps. Rotate the model 180°.

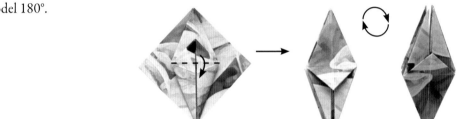

7 Pull the two petals apart, then tuck the triangular piece to the inside. Flatten along existing creases.

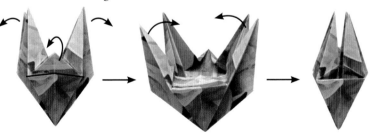

8 Repeat step 7 with the remaining sides.

55

9 This model requires an extra petal. Valley fold along the dashed line. Then pull the outer layer out and invert, flattening along existing creases.

10 Fold the extra petal up as shown.

11 Valley fold along the dashed lines shown and then push the petal tip down. Press out remaining petals.

12 Push the corner between regular petals down, using an inside reverse fold. Make a similar inside reverse fold on the corner opposite.

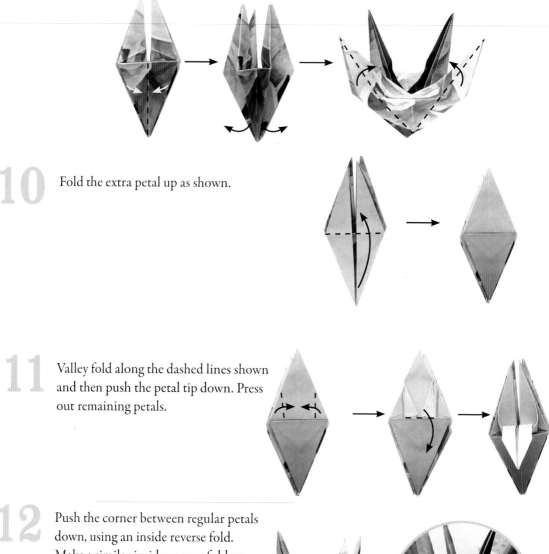

13 Squeeze the tip of the flower from all angles to narrow.

14 Curl the petals outward by rolling them around a pencil.

Christmas Cactus

1 Start with a blintz base, folded through step 2 (see page 7). Turn the model over. Fold the square into a preliminary base. The cut edges should be visible on the outer flaps.

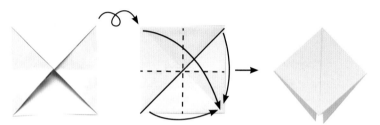

2 Book fold the right flap so that it stands up. Press the corner down and squash it flat.

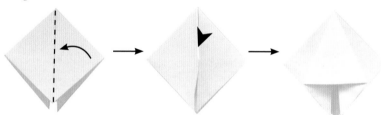

3 Valley fold the edges to the center and unfold.

4 Pull point A out and up, then flatten along existing creases.

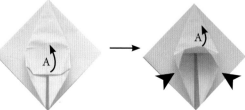

5 Fold the triangular piece down. Repeat steps 2 to 5 on the other three flaps.

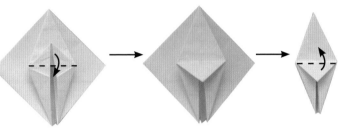

6 Pull the petals apart, then tuck the triangular piece to the inside. Flatten along existing creases.

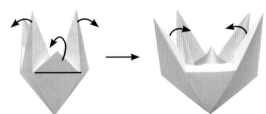

7 Repeat with the remaining petals.

8 This model requires extra petals. Make the first: fold along the dashed line, then pull the outer layer out and invert, flattening along existing creases.

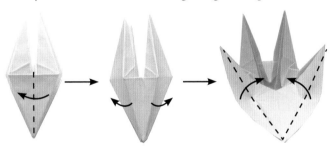

9 Repeat step 8 on the other sides to make a total of four extra petals.

10 Book fold the right flap to the left. Valley fold the bottom tip up part way.

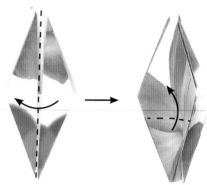

11 Repeat to valley fold the remaining petals.

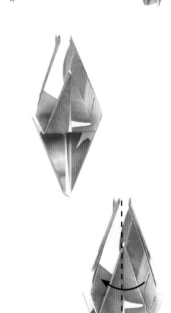

12 Book fold the top right flap to the left and book fold the bottom left flap to the right.

13 Valley fold the flaps toward the center. Repeat with the remaining flaps.

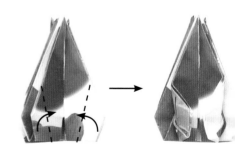

14 Book fold the top right flap to the left. Curl the petal outward by rolling it up around a pencil.

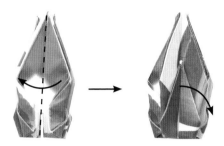

15 Repeat with remaining outer petals.

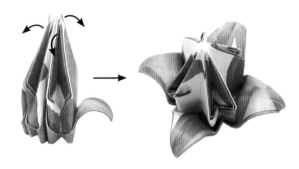

16 Curl the inner petals out part way. Attach leaf (see next page).

Christmas Cactus Leaf

1 Mountain fold along the diagonals and unfold, then turn the paper over.

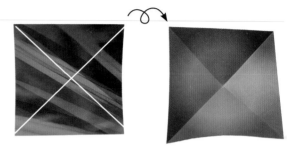

2 Valley fold the corners to the center crease.

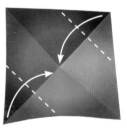

3 Valley fold the edges to the center crease. Then valley fold the edges to the center crease once more.

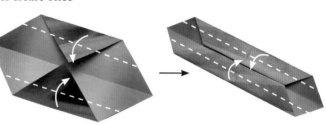

4 Fold the model in half from tip to tip, then fold each side in half (tip to center crease). Unfold after each fold.

5 Make an inside reverse fold on each edge, top and bottom. Make two more inside reverse folds along the top and bottom edges as shown.

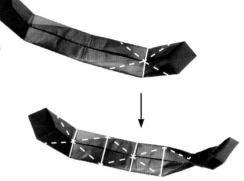

6 Fold a piece of floral stem wire to the same length as the leaf. Insert the wire between the layers; you can use tape on the inside to keep the wire in place.

7 Using instant-grab, fast-drying glue, affix a flower to the leaf tip.

Daffodil

1. Start with a blintz base (see page 7). Valley fold along the dashed lines shown. Turn the model over.

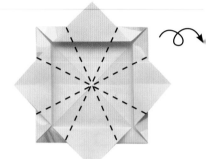

2. Start to collapse the model: fold points A and B to point C, alternating mountain and valley folds. Continue in this fashion until the model is flat and diamond shaped (see next step).

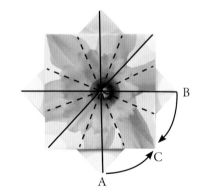

3. Valley fold as shown, then reverse the crease to a mountain fold for sharpness. Unfold the model to the view in step 2.

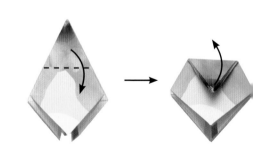

4 Mountain fold along existing creases, then press the center down to sink it.

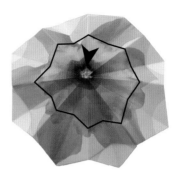

5 Press inward between the points while sharpening the mountain creases to flatten the model.

6 Book fold the flap a little to work on the corner.

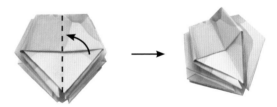

7 Inside reverse fold along the folding guides shown, pressing the new folds together firmly. Repeat on remaining flaps.

8 Pull the petal tip up to make an inside reverse fold.

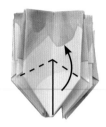

9 Repeat step 9 on five more petals in a row. The last two will not be folded this way.

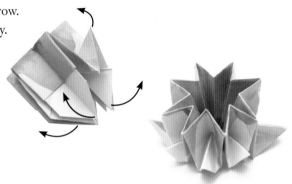

10 Fold the last two petals together in consecutive valley folds to lock in place.

11 View of the folded up petals. Turn the model over.

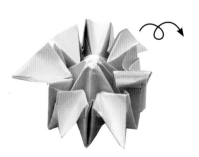

12 Flute out the edges of the flower's trumpet: make shallow inside reverse folds all around.

13 This is where the extra petals are folded together on the other side. Mountain fold the corners together to secure. Then press each petal flat with your fingers.

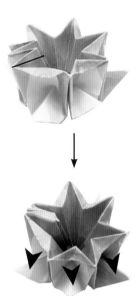

Iris

1. Start with a blintz base (see page 7) folded through step 2. Turn the model over. Fold the square into a preliminary base. The cut edges should be visible on the outer flaps.

2. Book fold the right flap so it stands up. Press the corner down and squash it flat.

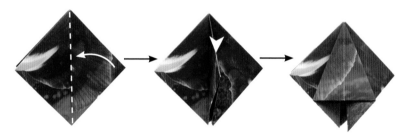

3. Valley fold the edges to the center and unfold.

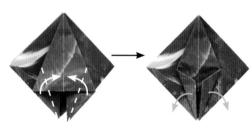

4. Pull point A out and up, then flatten along existing creases. Fold the small triangular piece down.

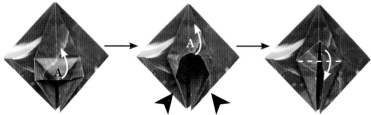

5 Repeat steps 2 to 4 on the other three flaps.
Rotate model 180°.

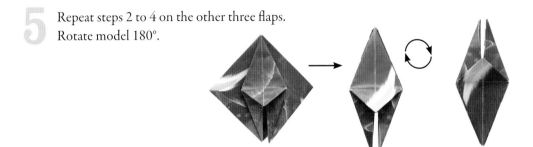

6 Pull the two petals apart, then tuck the triangular piece to the inside. Flatten
along existing creases. Repeat with the remaining sides.

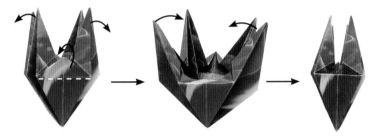

7 This model requires extra petals. Make the first: valley fold along the dashed
line. Then pull the outer layer out and invert, flattening along existing creases.

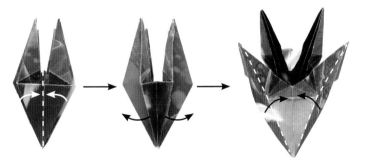

8 Fold the extra petal up as shown. Repeat on
two other sides of the model to make a total
of three extra petals. Turn the model over.

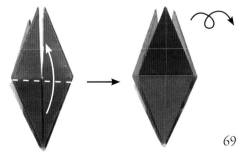

9 Book fold the right flap to the left. Four of the petals have more layers than the other three. Fold a thicker petal down. Now the model has six petals; the thinner three will be on the inside of the flower.

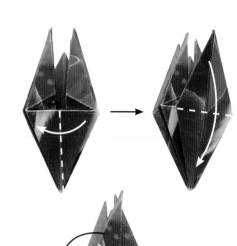

10 Mountain fold the petal as shown. Make a mirror image of the same fold on the other side of the petal. (Make sure this is one of the thicker petals.)

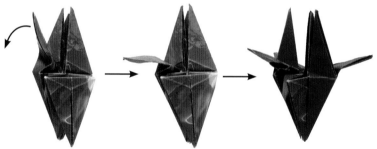

11 Press the folded petal out as shown. Repeat steps 9 to 11 on the other two thick petals.

12 Repeat step 10 on the thin petals, but do not press them out.

13 Mountain fold the tip of a thin petal.

14 Make another mountain fold on the tip of the same petal. Repeat steps 13 and 14 on the other thin petals.

15 Make an inside reverse fold on a thick petal tip. Press the tip down between the layers. Repeat with remaining thick petals.

Lily

1 Start with a blintz base (see page 7) folded through step 2. Turn the model over.

2 Fold the square into a preliminary base (see page 6). The cut edges should be visible on the outer layers.

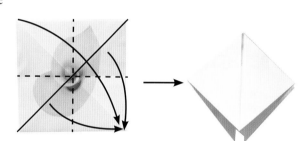

3 Book fold the flap on the right so it stands up. Press the corner down and squash it flat.

4 Valley fold the edges to the center crease and unfold.

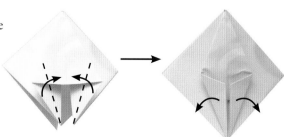

5 Pull point A out and up, then flatten along existing creases. Fold the small triangular piece down.

6 Repeat steps 3 to 5 on the other three flaps.

7 Rotate model 180°.

8 Pull the two petal tips apart as shown. Fold the triangular flap to the inside of the model. Flatten along existing creases.

9 Repeat with the remaining sides.

10 Valley fold along the dashed line. Pull the top layer out and invert. Flatten along existing creases. This makes a fifth petal.

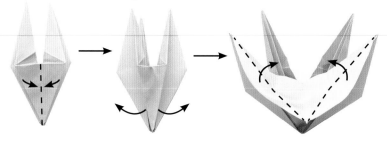

11 Fold this petal up. Valley fold the corner between petals, then fold back the adjacent corner of the next petal.

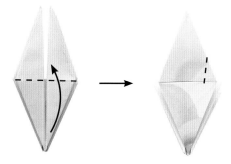

12 Press the corner layers flat. On the inside, press the paper between the petals flat to ease the tension.

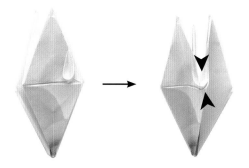

13 Repeat steps 11 and 12 on the other side of the extra petal. Turn the model to work on the remaining petals.

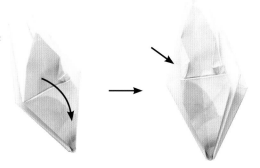

14 Make separations between other petals: fold
back the corners at the base of each flap.

15 Valley fold the inner corners between the
petals to lock them together and give the
flower shape.

16 Curl each of the five petals outward around
a pencil.

Narcissus

1. Start with a blintz base (see page 7), folded through step 2. Turn the model over. Fold the square into a preliminary base. The cut edges should be visible on the outer flaps.

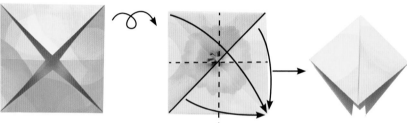

2. Book fold the right flap so that it stands up. Press the corner down and squash it flat.

3. Valley fold the edges to the center and unfold.

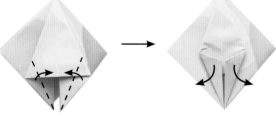

4. Pull point A out and up, then flatten along existing creases.

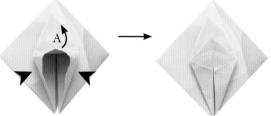

5 Fold the triangular piece down. Repeat steps 2 to 5 on the other three flaps. Rotate the model 180°.

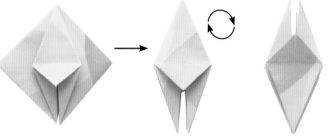

6 Pull the two petals apart, then tuck the triangular piece to the inside. Flatten along existing creases. Repeat with the remaining sides.

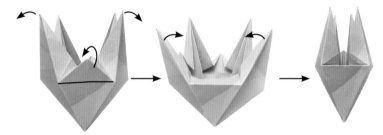

7 This model requires extra petals. Make the first: valley fold along the dashed line, then pull the outer layer out and invert, flattening along existing creases.

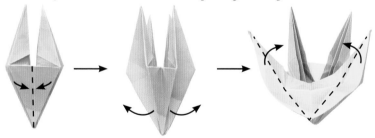

8 Fold the extra petal up. Turn the model over. Repeat on the other side.

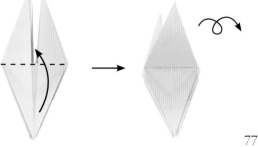

9 Now there are a total of six petals. Valley fold along the dashed line then mountain fold along the same crease to sharpen. Unfold.

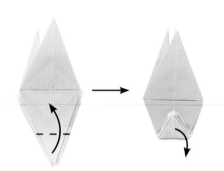

10 Flatten the model and mountain fold along existing creases. Push the center down to sink it.

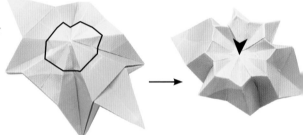

11 Collapse the model: press inward as shown so it folds up like an accordion. Flatten.

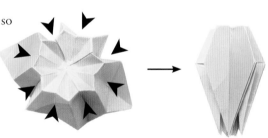

12 Inside reverse fold the top petal by pulling the tip up, then book folding point A to point B. Repeat with the remaining petals.

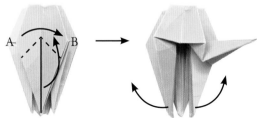

13 Mountain fold the corners of the petal shown. Repeat with the remaining petals.

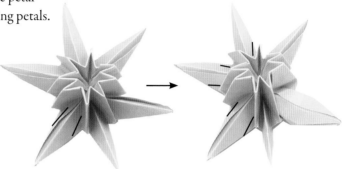

14 Mountain fold the edges shown to lock one side of the trumpet together.

15 Repeat with the edges on the opposite side.

16 Shape the edges of the trumpet: press down point C into an inside reverse fold to flute it.

17 Shape remaining edges in this fashion, except where the model was folded in steps 14 and 15. Valley fold these corners down.

18 Continue fluting edges of the trumpet outward.

19 Fold back the tip of each petal, then pinch each tip between two fingers to shape.